T0130545

A Canada Catastrophe

COLOURED VERSION

CHILDREN SAVING OUR PLANET SERIES

CAROL SUTTERS

AuthorHouse™ UK
1663 Liberty Drive
Bloomington, IN 47403 USA
www.authorhouse.co.uk
UK TFN: 0800 0148641 (Toll Free inside the UK)
UK Local: 02036 956322 (+44 20 3695 6322 from outside the UK)

This book is printed on acid-free paper.

ISBN: 978-1-6655-8801-0 (sc)
ISBN: 978-1-6655-8802-7 (e)

Library of Congress Control Number: 2021906643

Print information available on the last page.

Published by AuthorHouse 04/22/2021

authorHOUSE®

The family are at home in the lounge.

Dad announces, *"You can bring together much of your learning if we discuss the catastrophe in Canada with the Athabasca Glacier and the Jasper National Park, in the Rocky Mountains in Canada. We can watch a programme about this."*

The family are sitting around the television. The programme explains that the Athabasca Glacier is part of an icefield in the Canadian Rocky Mountains. Due to climate change warming, it loses more than 5 metres depth per year and it has lost over half of its volume of ice in the past 125 years. The Canadian icefield has warmed up twice as fast as other parts of the world.

Mum exclaims, "*This is tragic as many people rely on melting glaciers in Spring as a source of drinking water. What will happen when all the ice is lost and water dries up?*"

"*That's correct,*" says Tom. "*The reporter said in the Himalayas in Asia up to 2 billion people rely on the melting waters from ice for drinking water.*"

They learn that the Athabasca Glacier has been adversely affected by the higher temperatures caused by soot getting onto the ice. The soot makes the ice darker, which means it absorbs more heat from the sun and so it warms up and melts.

Kate questions, *"Where did the soot come from?"* Mum replies, *"From the nearby Jasper National Park. This happened as the climate there has warmed."*

Mum continues, *"The Jasper National Park is special because it is the largest national park in the Canadian Rockies. It spans across the Rocky Mountains and it is also a huge ecosystem of wildlife of plants and animals. Some of the small animals in Jasper Park include squirrels, marmots, beavers, weasels and porcupines. Larger animals include moose, deer, mountain goats, sheep, elk, cougars and black grizzly bears."*

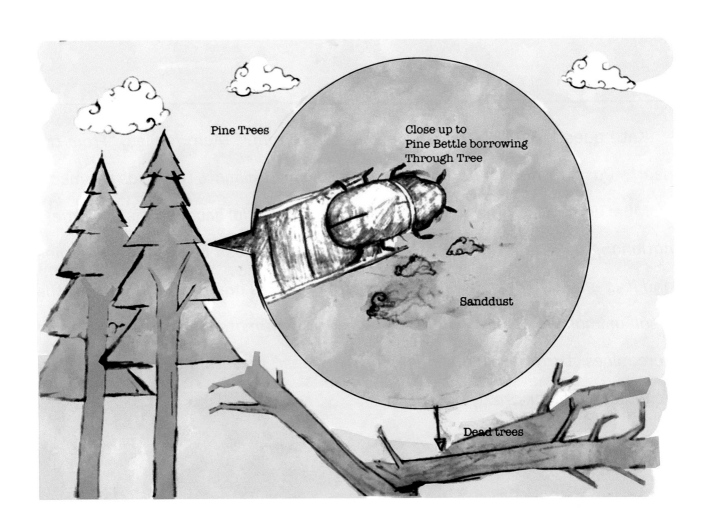

Pine Trees

Close up to
Pine Bettle borrowing
Through Tree

Sanddust

Dead trees

"The mountain pine beetles there, which used to die off in the cold winter season, now survive and attack the pine trees in Jasper National Park. The mountain pine beetle burrows into the pine tree bark and lays eggs under the bark. The developing eggs hatch and larvae feed from the trees under the bark. This turns the trees red and they die."

"*The pine trees try to defend themselves against the pine beetle. The pine trees make a resin to drown out the beetle but the trees have lost the battle against such large numbers of beetles that now survive. The mountain beetles cut off the pine trees food supply and water and this can happen in as little as two to four weeks in warmer months.*"

Mum says, "This is called a TIPPING POINT, which is a point of no return on the change. The result is that the original green pine trees have gone red-brown and grey and completely lost their needles and they eventually die. Dead dry trees mean that when wildfires start, the mountain pine trees burn easily and the soot gets carried in the air to the nearby glacier."

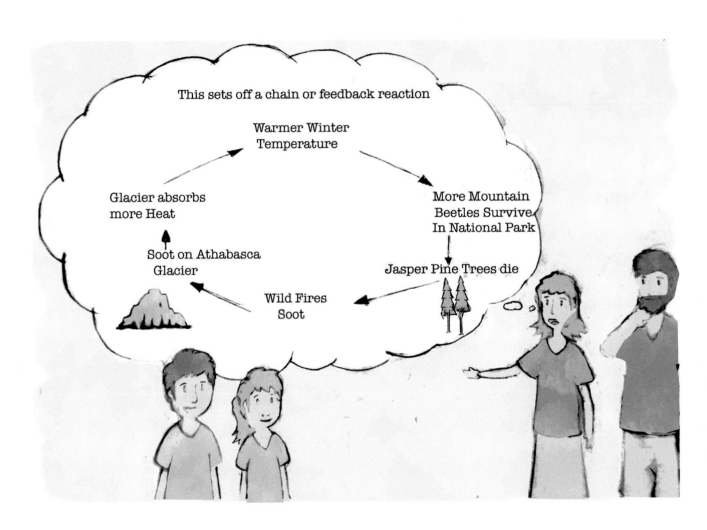

This sets off a chain or feedback reaction:

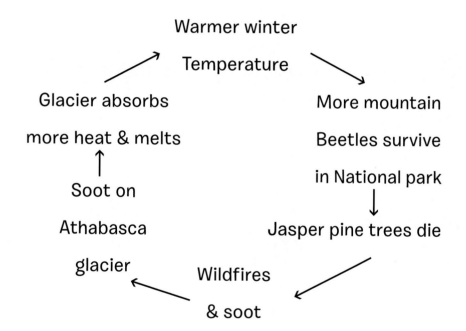

Warmer winter

Temperature

Glacier absorbs

more heat & melts

Soot on

Athabasca

glacier

Wildfires

& soot

More mountain

Beetles survive

in National park

Jasper pine trees die

What did we learn today? (tick the box if you understood and agree)

☐ The Canadian Jasper National Park is a large ecosystem of many wild animals and plants which needs to be preserved.

☐ The Athabasca Glacier is melting rapidly and it is due to climate change.

☐ The glacier effects are caused by changing the ecosystem in nearby Jasper pine forest. One system affects the other and this is an example of a feedback loop causing destruction of natural habitats.

☐ The warmer climate means the mountain pine beetle now survives in large numbers in Jasper Natural Park and destroys the pine trees.

☐ The dry pine trees are tinder for local forest fires which commonly occur in such dry conditions. The soot is carried by wind and collects on the Athabasca icesheet, causing it to warm and melt.

- [ ] We need to avoid getting to a Tipping Point in climate change when we destroy wildlife and the planet. At this crucial point, we lose the ability to reverse or cause less damage.
- [ ] Under normal conditions, when marginal parts of glaciers melt in Spring and produce waterfalls, this provides a useful source of water for some people.

Find out what Kate and Tom learn about Coronavirus and Saving the Planet in book 15.

Children Saving our Planet Series

Books

1. **Tom and Kate Go to Westminster**

2. **Kate and Tom Learn About Fossil Fuels**

3. **Tom and Kate Chose Green Carbon**

4. **Tress and Deforestation**

5. **Our Neighbourhood Houses**

6. **Our Neighbourhood Roads**

7. **Shopping at the Farm Shop**

8. **Travelling to a Holiday by the Sea**

9. **Picnic at the Seaside on Holiday**

These series of simple books explain the landmark importance of Children's participation in the Extinction rebellion protest. Children actively want to encourage and support adults to urgently tackle both the Climate and the Biodiversity emergencies. The booklets enable children at an early age to understand some of the scientific principles that are affecting the destruction of the planet. If global political and economic systems fail to address the climate emergency, the responsibility will rest upon children to save the Planet for themselves.

This series is dedicated to

Theodore, Aria and Ophelia.

Printed in the United States
by Baker & Taylor Publisher Services